Arghya Ray

Major Emphases of Sociological Enquiry in the Realm of Business Economics

GRIN Verlag

Bibliografische Information der Deutschen Nationalbibliothek:

Die Deutsche Bibliothek verzeichnet diese Publikation in der Deutschen National-
bibliografie; detaillierte bibliografische Daten sind im Internet über http://dnb.d-
nb.de/ abrufbar.

Imprint:

Copyright © 2009 GRIN Verlag GmbH
Druck und Bindung: Books on Demand GmbH, Norderstedt Germany
ISBN: 978-3-656-57551-1

This book at GRIN:

http://www.grin.com/en/e-book/231665/major-emphases-of-sociological-enquiry-
in-the-realm-of-business-economics

GRIN - Your knowledge has value

Der GRIN Verlag publiziert seit 1998 wissenschaftliche Arbeiten von Studenten, Hochschullehrern und anderen Akademikern als eBook und gedrucktes Buch. Die Verlagswebsite www.grin.com ist die ideale Plattform zur Veröffentlichung von Hausarbeiten, Abschlussarbeiten, wissenschaftlichen Aufsätzen, Dissertationen und Fachbüchern.

Visit us on the internet:

http://www.grin.com/

http://www.facebook.com/grincom

http://www.twitter.com/grin_com

Major Emphases of Sociological Enquiry in the Realm of Business Economics

By

Arghya Ray

Introduction

Sociology and economics have been regarded as two distinct and diverse subjects in the realm of social sciences. Although both of these subjects are about understanding the society, sociologists and economists differ in a number of ways on a number of issues of debate. For example, sociological studies are more dependent on empirical research and often involve considerable amount of fieldwork and collection of data. On the other hand, economics is more dependent on theory based mathematical deductions, although economic implications are extensively examined in the realm of business and commerce. However, with the lapse of time, it has become increasingly clear that in order to obtain a holistic view of society, both sociological and economic information are necessary. Therefore, in the mid 20th century, several scholars started working on economic issues from strictly sociological perspective. In this way, economic entities like the household, the firm, and the government are now being looked into with relation to people and the society at large. Business organisations are particularly important because they can be though of as quasi-social structures that do not always strictly behave according as well established economic formulas, theories, and doctrines. Sociologists are now utilising a number of academic and research approaches to understand business entities more comprehensively. In this essay, the most important sociological approaches are discussed concisely.

Discussion

According to Weber (1922), economic activities depend on three types of decisions. Rational decisions are well reasoned and most expected. Traditional decisions are those which are influenced by culture, practices, stereotypes, etc. Speculative-irrational decisions are those which are most difficult to predict and often incomprehensible with the help of standard economic theories. From a stricter point of view, even traditional decisions can be regarded as irrational in the sense that economic theories are insufficient to explain an individual's infatuation for traditions even at the cost of economic well being. In the wake of these complexities, researchers have attempted to use sociological perspectives and empirical techniques to explain decisions taken by individuals or groups in a complex business environment.

Networks Approach

In analyzing today's industrial world, a society can be regarded as a complex structure of various substructures that cater to various human activities. So this complex lattice of different institutions can be perceived as to have developed a multifarious network inside it. (Nohria and Eccles 1992; Block 1990)

This gigantic multifarious network has smaller and diverse networks inside it, which are intricately interconnected with each other. And the networks approach of studying sociology can be applied to understand and analyze the links that establish these networks. These links connect corporations, individuals, industries and even entire economies. Consequently, the networks approach is somewhat supple since in this approach the sociologist has to recognize the uniqueness of each and every network entity, although these entities are deemed interdependent. (Nohria and Eccles 1992)

View of the society as an inter-network of networks puts emphasis on the need of quantitative analysis to understand social functions and activities. In this way, networks approach has emerged as a pillar of economic sociology. It facilitates the analysis of interconnections between organizations and individuals. (Burt 1983)

Markets Approach

Markets approach attributes the study of sociology of markets. So in this realm of sociological enquiry, the whole emphasis is on the markets. Yet, unlike economists, sociologists have to understand that how other components of the society influence or interact with the markets. In the realm of economic discourse, sociology of markets has been widely recognized. Yet, mathematical models used by economists often neglect the complex sociological factors in understanding customer behaviour. (Block 1990; Barber 1977)

In the markets approach, phenomena related to the differential powers of various market agents are studied. Instead of labelling incomprehensibilities of customer behaviour as irrationalities, sociology of markets is aimed at explaining them with the help of socio-economic factors that are deeply entrenched in the society at large. (Burt 1982)

Corporations Approach

The rise of giant corporations has led many sociologists think that the modern industrial society has intricate relationships with the powerful corporations as far as socio-economic activities are concerned. Large corporations can change the economic, and hence, the social situation too of a locality by providing people with employment, products, economic opportunities, etc. So these trends can be attributed to the new institutional economics, where political forces such as governments are not the sole decision makers. Hence, the emphasis of sociological study is put on the structure and function of corporations. (Williamson 1975)

However, the uniqueness of corporations approach lies in the fact that it is aimed at the internal structure of a corporation along with its various externalities. It is true that the society is affected mainly be a corporation's interaction with the various social structures like banks and governments. Yet, the corporation's internal structure should also be studied so that its attitude towards the society can be understood better. So the corporations approach puts considerable emphasis on studying the internal structure, culture, and management of corporations. Business historians like Chandler (1981) have argued that firms with multiple departments and divisions develop since they behave in economically rational ways. Rise of giant corporations is explained on the basis of organizational skills and coherence that result into successful organizational cultures. Sociologists attempt to link such organizational behaviour with broader social behaviour.

Conclusion

If modern sociologists do not emphasise research on economic aspects of the society, a wholesome understanding of social activities, interactions and processes cannot be harnessed. In the wake of globalisation, economics and industry have become more dependent on mighty corporations. It is neither possible nor wise to neglect the corporations as semi-social structures becoming more and more powerful everyday. Not only corporations approach but also networks and markets approach have focussed on the socio-behavioural dynamics of corporate entities, which are mostly privately owned bodies. Likewise, economic actions of individuals too are not isolated events but can be viewed as have been arranged inside social networks influenced by political and advertising campaigns. In sum, the future of sociology will largely depend on the current areas of emphasis where research is aimed at examining the global business environment as intricately as possible.

References

Barber, B. (1977), The absolutization of the market: Some notes on how we got from there to here. In: G. Dowkin, G. Bermant, and P. Brown (Eds.), *Markets and Morals*, Washington D.C.: Hemisphere, pp. 15-31

Block, F. (1990), Economic sociology. In: *Post Industrial Possibilities: A Critique of Economic Discourse*, Berkeley: University of California Press, pp. 21-45

Burt, R. (1983), *Corporate Profits and Cooperation: Networks of Market Constraints and Directorate Ties in the American Economy*, New York: Academic Press

Chandler, A.D. (1981), Historical determinants of managerial hierarchies. In: A. Van de Ven and J. Joyce (Eds.), *Perspectives on Organisational Design*, New York: Wiley, pp. 391-402

Nohria, N. and Eccles, R. (1992), *Networks and Organisations: Structure, Form, and Action*, Boston: Harvard Business School

Weber, M. (1922), *Economy and Society: An Outline of Interpretive Sociology.*
Berkeley: University of California Press, 1978

Williamson, O. (1975), *Markets and Hierarchies: Analysis and Antitrust Implications*,
New York: Free Press